PRAISE FOR *CREVASSE*

Nicholas Wong's *Crevasse* inhabits the fiery crossroads that connect sexuality, masculinity, language, and race — a radical space that challenges the stubbornly trite assumptions about queer and Asian identities. His poems shape a fierce voice — techno savvy and street smart, sophisticated and politically charged — which allows the reading journey to coast from witty to wise, frequently turning the corner into poignant and provocative. What an exhilarating book! — RIGOBERTO GONZÁLEZ

Nicholas Wong is a poet of the body, and for him even the poem is a body. In *Crevasse*, the poems breathe and hunger and drink. They are after what all human bodies want: life, vitality. Or as Wong himself puts it, "Every death is a local event every local/avoids..." Line to line, these poems juxtapose all a body touches; this is a book of action. — DEMERY, JERICHO BROWN

"Uncircumscribed poets/believe madly in/breadth, depth, spaciousness,/the atomic brain," Nicholas Wong writes in *Crevasse*. In poems that career, collide, and collage, Wong makes use of multiple discourses while also confronting them. This is poetry that is unashamed to be relentless — *Crevasse* widens the eyes and restarts the heart. — TARFIA FAIZULLAH

Deftly cleft and radically inventive, Nicholas Wong's *Crevasse* blows a hole right through our expectation of what contemporary poetry is supposed to look and to sound like, offering us a surprising celebration of and elegy for our disposable, sanctified bodies. Wong anagrams "capitalism" into "I am plastic," seduces us with "jargons that renew the old curve," and provides us with "hand-made happiness" that resonates like few new books do. Full of wit, but never glib, spectacularly sexual but never profane, deeply intelligent but never ostentatious, this book is a genuine revelation, providing us with erasures, adaptations, and mistranslations that are urgent and essential, and rendered in an unmistakeable style, a memorable voice all his own. Nicholas Wong is the future of poetry, and with the publication of *Crevasse*, that future is now. — RAVI SHANKAR

CREVASSE

For information about permission to reproduce selections from this book,
please write to permissions@kaya.com.

Published by Kaya Press
www.kaya.com

Cover and book design by Jason Bacasa

Distributed by D.A.P. / Distributed Art Publishers
155 Avenue of the Americas, 2nd Floor, New York, NY 10013
800.338.BOOK www.artbook.com

Library of Congress Cataloging-in-Publication Data
Wong, Nicholas, 1979 –
[Poems. Selections]
Crevasse / by Nicholas Wong.
pages cm
Includes bibliographical references.
ISBN: 978-1-885030-20-7
I. Title.
PR9450.9.W65A6 2015
823'.92--dc23
2015002901

Printed in the United States of America

This publication is made possible by support from the USC Dana and David Dornsife College of Arts,
Letters, and Sciences; the USC Department of American Studies and Ethnicity; and the USC Asian
American Studies Program. Kaya Press is funded in part by the Los Angeles Board of Supervisors through
the Los Angeles County Arts Commission. Special thanks to the Choi Chang Soo Foundation for their
support of this work. Additional funding was provided through the generous contributions of Lily &
Tom Beischer, Lisa Chen & Andy Hsiao, Floyd & Sheri Cheung, Jim Chu, Prince Gomolvilas, Jean Ho, Huy
Hong, Juliana S. Koo, Whakyung Lee, Ed Lin, Noriko Murai, Viet Thanh Nguyen, Gene & Sabine Oishi,
Chez Bryan Ong, Thaddeus Rutkowski, Anantha Sudhakar, Patricia Miye Wakida, Duncan Williams,
Amelia Wu & Sachin Adarkar, Anita Wu & James Spicer, and others.

CREVASSE

NICHOLAS WONG

KAYA PRESS
LOS ANGELES • NEW YORK

"... my body itself is a thing, which I do not observe: in order to be able to do so, I should need the use of a second body which itself would be unobservable."

— MAURICE MERLEAU-PONTY

CONTENTS

Private Parts: Anti-Bodies / **13**

Meditations on How to Break up with My Sick Boyfriend / **14**

Nono (Uncorrected Proof) / **15**

Unspeakable / **16**

Metro Public Bodies / **18**

Postcolonial Zoology / **19**

Self-Portrait as Eeyore, To Pooh / **20**

MR. / **21**

Physiognomy / **23**

Orientalism / **24**

If We Are a Metaphor of the Universe / **26**

Private Parts: American Standard / **29**

Archipelago / **30**

Trio with Hsia Yü / **31**

Star Gazing / **34**

Match Point / **35**

Inside Heterosexuality: Notes on Non-Human Resources / **36**

Abandonment Combo / **37**

Neighbor / **38**

Aqua / **41**

Side Effects of Leukemia / **43**

Self-Portrait as a Cubicle / **45**

I Love to Be Your Witness / **47**

Five Steps on Expository Writing: Origin of Hydrophilia / **50**

Self-Portrait as Salmon Roe at Revolving Sushi / **51**

Private Parts / **52**

Minor Bodies, or Me Embedded in 3, 5, or 7 Words / **53**

Open House / **55**

A Very Personal Reflection on My Lesson about *Lord of the Flies* / **56**

Museum of Anagapesis / **58**

Schuyler Haikus, 1954-58 / **59**

How to Refund Your Identity / **71**

Light Deposit / **73**

Notes / **75**

Acknowledgements / **76**

PRIVATE PARTS: ANTI-BODIES

Born as a suckling machine, hooked
to nipples on malevolent male
chests, where hair grows like black grass
in barren deserts. Inside me a groove
deepens, which I have mistaken
for love. My therapist says *Be alone, the gap will
heal.* As if *alone* were a persona.
To be alone is to be someone else, to reject
paired objects: chopsticks, socks,
movie sequels. My nose, my heart
breathing and beating in solo are the world's
bravest singletons, I should learn from them.
Is this how hermits become hermits? When pity
pinches their organs, they cut
open their bowels with a sword to see
what solitude looks like. It looks like
the mouth of their caves, the lips
I have kissed, slightly parted like the cowboy's
in a cigarette ad. Or a honeysuckle,
blossoming, anthers curling
upward, petals pitifully apart.

MEDITATIONS ON HOW TO BREAK UP WITH MY SICK BOYFRIEND

What is it that you want to say? *Strop, Systole*
or *Strumpet?* Stolen is your speech by the sly air,

which does what it does even when health prevails.
Do they still mention health in the vow? *In sickness and in*

fact, you are filling our room with cacophonies of coughing,
a viral symphony. A blanket against your chest, you think

perhaps about antihistamine, but if antibodies are loyal
(or specific) in choosing what to be against,

why are you against monogamy? I have found you
chicken soup with alphabets floating like defeated

troops. With a spoon, you sieve an E after a W,
which I think is an M upside down. You insist,

swallow the word, get choked on it.

NONO (UNCORRECTED PROOF)

Double Illegitimacy: a colloquial term coined in 2012 to refer to newborns
in Hong Kong whose parents are both of illegal status within the city

Me is no/ sperm   no egg/   me is out

rage of both/   me is hiccup   betwin

lunguage and deficit/   Diu means

fuck/ Diu to me five star flag   me tongue can

not say "th"   in the in them in nothing

in theater   me hand has no/ other hand but me

other hand to touch   *diu*/ in theater   me is movie

ticket stub/   stubborn popcorn

seed unpopped/ papa   do you know me

Chinese name has many   meaning/ mean double

no   double fly/ like butter

fly lover in theater   mean two woman four hand

arrive at happy   ending/ why mama begin

begging like other mama before this

building/   mama is need is noisy   mama yell

hum with other nono/ other   banner *no milk no school*

no bed in sea   of baby eye/   black

but tiny like sea of sesame   dust of/ten mistake

Mamihlapinatapai 1. Your mommy loves you not/ like a pie, but I do. 2. I bake/ you, break you into crusts. 3. The oven, our witness.   *Schadenfreude* 1. A skin to fight with. 2. Desire/ to infect you with my history, though history/ manifests itself as disinfectant in textbooks. 3. There're nights I slept some-where else & returned, reeking/ of cheaper bed sheets. 3.1. "Keep/yourself as an/ other. Keep your seduction/ alive." I   *Desenrascanço* [cont'd] con-soled you with triplets of loaded end/ rhymes. 2. I tatter the trachea, am bored with bronchitis, its inflammatory notion of twoness. 3. Three is better. *Ilunga* 1. "The deepest part of lungs ready to/ forgive any abuse for the first time,/ to tolerate it a second time, but never/ a third time." 2. A seismograph in/ hopes of stillness.   *Bakku- shan* 1. A croissant in hopes of seeing/ the melting face of butter.   *Pochemuchka* 1. Electrocution by Pokémon for the felony/ of adultery. 1.1. Pets ask/ lots of questions, they don't/ age. 2. They like you & you,/ like them, need the "illusion/ of the world" & of your life.   *Duende* 1. The way I rode you like a Volvo.   *Backpfeifenge-sicht* 1. A box of physicians thinking/ outside the box, as in there's gravity because there's/ grief. 2. Grief hears speeches slowed/ down by hiccups. 3. A throat sinks/ in the muscularity of the chest: Who/ needs evidence in thoracic science?   *Gigil* 1. The keys I used to open your sliding doors. *L'esprit de l'escalier* 1. A spirit that kills metaphors with metaphors. 2. At the therapist, you saw yourself/ as a camel & me as rocks hoarded in humps. 3. I was detritus at worst. 3.1 a sharp/ spirit that jilted.   *Litost* 1. The loss of light in the plainest prison.   *Waldeinsamkeit* 1. Language is kind as hooklets. 2. It causes/ the least pain of un-understanding. 3. Your far-flung shadow will one day swing back like a turnstile with self-/ erasing rage. 4. This is the least I pray for.   *Hyggelig* 1. Who commiserates/ hyacinth wreathed & uprooted/ with gruffness? 2. The point of flowers/ is the scent, never the plants. 3. The perfect rhyme of hyena is me.   *Yoko meshi* 1. Solitude "induced by speaking/ a foreign language." 2. Lips being kissed sideways. 3. How much hair breaks in a sleep unnecessarily slept? 1.1 Solitude spoken (of)/ like a *lingua franca*. I need a dictionary that translates it.

That girl with a Mohawk is fingering
the slot machine on her iPhone.

The jingle of virtual coins falling is godsend,
each of the same volume, same sharpness, never detuned.

An old man holding an Aiwa Walkman
with the speaker on replays fifteen seconds

of *Greensleeves*. Clicking of black plastic buttons
nestles nostalgia on buttocks of the present.

A mother urges her son to watch Siamese twins
on cabin TV. He laughs, pointing

at the uncanny. She says some people were born like *that* —
belly-blended, navel-less, the body over complete.

POSTCOLONIAL ZOOLOGY
1997, Hong Kong

It is not the pedigreed corgis they left
at the handover, but the effigy of the Queen
on toothed stamps being self-important

in dusted albums. We bolted to banks to trade
for new coins. We went to the West, away
from communist coxswains, but were whittled

to sculptures called "second-tier citizens,"
second to terriers. Our being could start
a chapter in zoology: we are inedible

bilingual centaurs spreading swine flu
at the turn of the century, we are comrades
of a blue whale found ashore due to sonic

confusion, caribous on a cruise to Malibu.
Even what we remembered migrated to corners
invisible in brain scans. In Mandarin Oriental,

India, a TV host devoured British scones
and circumscribed cucumber sandwiches
on his sun porch that looked over to rice fields.

A butler next to him. He called the experience
authentic. So were the bees buzzing in air,
sick of their queen too lazy to move.

SELF-PORTRAIT AS EEYORE, TO POOH

Thank you for ignoring me like a bridesmaid.
Each picture in this book a wedding

of you and the kids' gaze: your drool,
bouncy belly, the ever-spilling honey

you say you'll lick but never. Thank you
for treating me like a cardboard cutaway,

forever on the side, at the back, an eyesore
in the dim. Thank you, really, for the tail,

which isn't exactly a tail, but a scrap
tourniquet stitched up against my ass.

And the balloons I don't adore, stubborn
rubber yearning to rise in inelastic sky.

I know my fate. No one likes donkeys,
diligent ogres snoring over soiled plows.

Let's play hide and seek, let's play hide
and deceit. Find me inhumed in a landfill

by a seesaw, glooming the past and present,
as if there was always more to be fixed.

MR.

He taught me about empires, got spotted
in a ferry leaning almost too close to a man
in the same tee. People like us traveled a lot,

often with grist to unravel the abutments of risky
fabric, practiced the Barbarian Invasion, fought
from a hetero shore to the less hetero soil.

It was science when a boat floated. So was
it when one sank. Mass increased,
buoyancy gave in. His body knew it,

his liver a budded rival of his own cells,
pushing down the declivity every
historically healthy bit of him. I wished

the harbor wafts gentled his sallow skin
despite the waves and noisy seagulls.
My fault of smattering when Reformation

began, what was reformed. Of finding radio-
therapy more theatrical than Marie Antoinette.
He said his speech was unclear now, ball

point pens feckless, upside down in a mug,
unpaired. History not a mistake repeating but
a red smudgy rabbit stamp I once had for recounting

facts on time and exactly as he said.
The way he wrote *Renaissance* on the board was
so neat. I almost saw a straight line beneath.

PHYSIOGNOMY

There's a moment I nearly believe your dermis
is representational. Upper lip thicker

than the lower, you're a lifeboat of inflated
grief. Your eyebrows buoy suddenness too soaked to sink.

Your nose, tall like a flaw, nestles warmth. You're honest,
a retiree of redemption, have jobs decent

like definitions. I cross your nasal bridge, which
is just a nasal bridge. It's windy there, my fake

panache aches. If I were a nation of owlets,
I'd own you as my diplomat for your forehead

broad as a chopping board: sign of longevity.
What carved the short crow's feet? Your reluctance to shave

or your clutching onto foresight? Of course, bad eye
cream. Don't frown — I'll land on your jawbone with jargons

that renew the old curve. The face is a model,
a potential. I'll bring glue and meaning. A blue

swipes across your beard like karaoke lyrics.
I make myself your content when your face sings not.

ORIENTALISM

We grieved for Kim Jong Il. We had to
believe the country was a mute that had lots
of words to offer. We worked with cows,

ate them, then tree barks and human calves.
We peeled the muscles but kept the hearts
alive. In a country that had lots of humans

to offer, I married young. On honeymoon,
my wife and I stuck to one TV channel.
We had only one TV channel

about boundaries, where they ended and how,
in a way, the outside world also ended. One day,
we swam to China, where words swung

between siren | serenade, sorrow | surreal.
The water was deep, muddy, swirling.
My wife couldn't make it. I went

quiet like the border of this country that
offered itself as a *maybe* in a box, or maybe
a jade. Either way, lexemes were truncated —

a plunk of "dis-" from the neck of "quiet"
or "play." Either way, I guillotined my past below
my neck, fermented it. I bartered my kimchi

away for a second name: Sam Song. And a second wife,
though I miss the submissiveness of my first,
our proper poverty. A scar can archive

and achieve burning to crust in time
for a laugh. I'm happy now in this stillness
that shifts, they say, just the matter of time.

IF WE ARE A METAPHOR OF THE UNIVERSE

If on the verge I lure capitalism to sleep over

If selfhood is redeemable from shelves of condoms at 7-11

If I confuse packaged emotions with intentions

If this is why I was the water drop in my fourth-grade school play

If wishing emotions expired like anecdotes

If reality is best read with a fictional mindset and you know it

If on second thought capitalism rejects me to have more time and space

If on second thought I thought he was full of that time and space

If not catching the calm and the asking of his breath

If he recommends sleeping instead with politics

If politics is likely, as he says, more anatomical, showy and loud

If scandals only work with fame and I am not worried

If mixing the certification of the self with social science is not a fault

If a fault can be undone like I am undone

If we anagram capitalism to *I am plastic*

If the madness and madeness of recycling is self-contained

If it is more expensive to burn feelings than to buy them

If most things that can be bought are bought out of stillness

If things include stocks, children, companionship

If stillness costs

If lies are sponsored vernacular of truths

If they are they are they are are they and you know it

If a pulse in pusillanimity breaks from a continuum of beats

If lumpy initials of corporates laugh on swings invisibly

If it is natural to hear iron chains screech because the wind blows

If please remove me from the list

If listing lust on the walls of a tormented love shaft

If you see my love is a red, red hose

If setting foot on half a sky

If a frog in a well knows it has swum in creeks as a tadpole, unashamed

If the well suddenly wants to travel but what to take with its hollow torso

If a pulse is willing to pay a rainforest of commissions to have its own
thoughts

If torsos are towed to a compulsory stop

If flesh is a commitment to melancholy and the lack of interest in
connecting

If dice can do nothing, if days can do nothing

If citizenship is a menu of 15 courses

If it also makes this nice zip around your lips

PRIVATE PARTS: AMERICAN STANDARD

I whiten my morning into liquid
by having some milk

of human kindness. Walking reveals
one foot of the cruising, another

of the cruised. We make music with
our feet, our synchronous shoes. Out,

damned milk spot on my pants.
Out, damned hot stalker seeking weight

and wish near urinals, porcelains only
"American Stand-

ard" can approach. Unsex me here, I wish
I was not biological, but a machine sticky

as marzipan. My bending is a sorry sight,
teeming with shortage of esteem. Who cares —

the soap dispenser only speaks
to the wall. When his arms hold me

from behind, I know what
he wants, the pasteurized kind.

ARCHIPELAGO

We say no man is an island to keep bodies
away from carapace, arthritis from the world atlas.

Even when someone is an island, no one
has turned a body into a ferry, hairs into life jackets.

No life jackets on the island: the back is the largest
plateau to hang a tattoo, to hold demurrals.

Let's assume the island is then colonized.
Peacocks open a spectrum of feathers to a noise

and mate in a foreign way. A satellite scans the island,
defines the circularity. Semi-

closed eyelids also show trust. The island's population
grows as the self splits. The first self shawls itself

because the second self self-actualizes too much. Locals call
it *cukou*, meaning exit, or close enough, fouled mouth.

TRIO WITH HSIA YÜ

1

I entered the wrong room
and missed my reincarnation.

That baby kicked, cried, skin
so thin also transparent that

capillaries beneath revealed
the purple pumping of life.

I stood over the mother's
shoulder, seeing her kiss

the baby's forehead. That sound
of the lips should have been mine.

2

Use a pen to write on the body,
then use the body to unbind

the heart. Roll the heart
over a few pages of grammar

and see whose rules are cruder.
Use a ruler to assess the percentage

of atrium that averts the other,
then use it to outline a safety

zone. Undo what is done,
but don't draw in dotted lines.

You lost your childhood in an amusement
park. At the popcorn stand,

electric heat altered oval seeds
to irregularity. The clown said he ran

out of paper cones, so you ran
away from happiness. Even helium

fled from foil balloons, now flaccid
like red blood cells under a microscope.

You withdrew your faith in butter
and caramel, invested in karmas

and Buddhist cycles. You practiced
the art of stop loss, tried to retrieve

the loss in adulthood, in adultery.
My carotid crooked when you drilled a pole

into my skull and I became your carousel.

STAR GAZING

"It's my duty to take care of him." — Masaki Goh (? – 2013), *The AWL*

The porn star died the day the Yen dropped,
lots of drooping arrows on Bloomberg
as usual. As usual, I revived his arousal life
on X-tube. Deep in *When Strangers Meet*,
strangers met in the kenosis of sweat.
His skin crisscrossed skin of twin twinks, busy
leading with moving rubber and angle.
His elasticity, his last fatigue between *play*
and *stop*, stopped. I rewound —
The porn star died the day the Yen dropped,
lots of *iku / kimochi / kinky chin chin* and noun-
and-verb confusion between his legs.
That's hand-made happiness,
the hands aware of themselves.
Like most constellations', his birth
was more referential than narrative.
He played roles that liked to open
things. Tonight, a close-up was not
what neared in real. Come back, could not,
not even with his unbreakable hair
wax, not even after his breath was sucked
into a white dwarf or black hole.

MATCH POINT

Since when are my hands   coarse like hands that are
   not mine? Enough of rackets that   resemble other rackets and certain
parabolas of our flesh.   Enough   with the net of proud squares, a penumbral
barrier. We take sides,
so do geese,   whose left-winged feathers make the best badminton shuttles.
We hit one back and forth (despite deuce), back and   further to where   wafts
of sweat refuse our bodies   to dry like IKEA glassware.
Same-sex
     sportsmanship is promiscuous: each flick serve flings a curve to *love-*
    all, one-love or   *love*(d)*-one.* A topspin sometimes under-
spins, the shuttle falls outside   the sideline. A linesman   opens his arms, but don't
take him   as an allegorist. He makes space   to mean loss.

Irony is I count corners to survive.
Leaking turns of a tub, a door
wedge near a cobweb. I count on them.

How interesting lifts are faithful
only to the vertical. A sign says
In case of ~~lift~~ life breakdown,

press the button. Release. Speak —
My pet moth dismantles its wings
at dawn, it has found comfort

crawling on its crooked feet.
I am warm, I wear low-cut socks. My shoes
to cross thresholds, borders, and minds

are kept indoors, like shame, which smells
fresh, like sashimi. Call me *faggot*
I cannot swim anyway, my firecracker

vines grow sideways like drowning octopi
upside down. My German memento says
Glück, but moments always are too big

to be framed. I want simple, but details begin.
Fetishes are simply details. Give me AA batteries.
I carry a torch in broad daylight.

ABANDONMENT COMBO

In Smart Games, the joystick, too, long rusted for not being struck
anymore toward the down, then up, so Pac-man can't further his dot-

eating existence in a maze eased with four exits. Neither can Chun Li float
upside down, spread and swirl her turbo legs in her tight *cheongsam.*

But who still seeks those tokens stacked back to back, ready to game
over and again and what about the pleasure of dropping them, one by face-

less one through the cleavage below the waist of each machine? Outside,
the arcade sign stills, flickers, in hopes of re-trending, because trends usually

return, though this one doesn't. Lonely is the *start* button once touched like
a second self, the rough pixilated edges of Mario's head after it head-butts

a brick to find gold no longer falls for the blue collar, not like that.

NEIGHBOR

Every death is a local event every local

avoids. The way we zigzag our way
by the gate to avoid this spot the skull

has crushed then opened like a generous

guava. The way we think the chalked
outline of the victim, a man, hardly

synopsizes the outlined body we carry

thus know of. The way a tent is zipped
to eclipse his plunge from public talks

because he has taken another he too personally,

privately — the myth of love bisects these he's,
who wet their love for myths with well-meant selves.

Tomorrow, the street will reek of bleach,

will gray as if intolerant of red, and stories
of the spot be untold by bold tire tracks.

A wreath by the curb

tilts, an umbrella, unclaimed, waits
for better weather to disclose its ribs.

AQUA

After the quake
a crevasse —

what leaks into the air
like a moth
maniacal about

light

•

A clock's hand ticks
to hate the grid

between two
minutes, a frigid

distance of shook
and shock

•

Sacrilege — the land
is an embryo

outside a uterus

Survivors think
of the missing,

then the shape
of the missing

●

Let nature be

the new linguist —
Loss now

a count noun,
concrete

like beans

●

We, thinly

languaged, catalog
catastrophes,

a dozen disembodied
heads, one

for each month

SIDE EFFECTS OF LEUKEMIA

Who invented the body as a republic, but forgot
to dedicate its anthem to your chemo cuticle?

Some cells live alone, remember, you won't
see them. See no difference between

beauty and utility when your charts, tubes,
fingers are equally clinical.

Who came here before? Who went away
in your coming? Absence, at least and last,

becomes a metaphor that means a head,
re-virginized. You've lost all the hair

there is to lose, then know there're men
who, like you, manage to bald gracefully.

For weeks, you wake with borrowed marrow.
For weeks, you wish to flirt with the unknown

donor of this blood that infiltrates into the
phonics of lymphocytes. Try whiskey, try to find

a voice for your joke about the L word,
how it sounds like *ukulele*. You want music,

a tropical tan. You want your mother to
learn the word, its spelling,

not context. Holes are drilled around your
clavicle. You feel anatomical. Too often

the body needs wounds to be grateful for
intactness. Quarantine slides on your chin

like a triple blade, loneliness ingrown.

SELF-PORTRAIT AS A CUBICLE

Keep me clean —

that microbial oval toilet seat,
overused, turned

ivory with occasional
drips of yellow,

a Jackson Pollock
on periphery.

⬥

Keep me sanitized

says a sign — laminated
with ripped corners,

narrating how to spread
sterilizer evenly

around the curve.

⬥

Unbuckled, pants
down, knees
bent. Starts

the waiting for enclosed
ongoing.

•

On my body,
there are words,
drawings,

phone numbers. And
a hole,

small, but big enough
for your eye.

You peep
through it, a fecund

kaleidoscope
for a face-

less prepuce
cordoned off by me.

I LOVE TO BE YOUR WITNESS

How thirst does the work, then the eyes

How the whipped cream of a Frappuccino stands without lickable legs

How my eyes witness a straw behead the cream

How the cut is crude, but neat. And cutting casts pleasure hard to resist

How a beggar pleads outside

How his head lowers

How humility is landward

How my gaze rides on his back of eczema

How my gaze translates sleaze into pity, pity into power

How his becomes mine

How I need the power to feel good because I don't often

How my gaze returns to the other, so I won't be full of myself

How he keeps begging simple

How a cardboard says he'll bring coins to Mars to debug me

How I will become less infected

How I can avoid the night and its weird-if-not-fucked-up sense of ratio
and definition of skinniness

How victims are created to decorate peace

How I should say no to gamma rays

How I should botox existence until it blossoms

How sickles hammer and hammers hum

How not every note from a saxophone jazzes

How the reverse of white is return

How nations run out of colors for flags

How hope is six inches long and often needs replacement

How I should have loud speakers to see and feel the vibration of sounds

How savings accounts don't spatially exist though banks do

How my vision doubles without a cornea transplant

How me | him, separated by a madness hinge

How a hand ghosts, steadies within this me-him

How his sexuality is knife-ready

How he slices his sexuality, puts it into a blender, and drinks it like coffee
    every morning

FIVE STEPS ON EXPOSITORY WRITING:

By the pool, three toy ducks drool,
yellow plastic of S / M / L. I tell you love

1. Collect the most important information.

has no size if we're all sizes, all ducks, and you say true
love ungloves the body if humidity is 100%.

2. Explain unusual words or terms.

I dive in, my legs flutter kick, my arms mechanic
like windmills. I think of the gender of pool jets,
view the fisheye view of other swimmers' butts
and the world vividly curvy up there

3. Use enough details to thoroughly inform readers.

as if it's built by Gaudí. I fill a bucket
with water and empty it by the rain
shower drain just to prove what I can do besides
being the brackets in your habits.

4. Teach something new.

If next morning we wake up with breath bad
enough and you think of pillows instead of me,
I'll hide the towels and hairdryer, say
your legs are leaking conduits, and the space
they induce when bent in bed, a dry lagoon.

5 Make predictions.

SELF-PORTRAIT AS SALMON ROE AT REVOLVING SUSHI

My existence elevates a bit between buckwheat
noodles and squids. Despite this,
I can't rift the conveyor belt, my cosmos
of rejection. I'm over-gendered,
I'm female moons set in too much
motion, unfertilized kings-would-be
stuck in a sticky rice throne, in which
there's craft. A fist of rice
gripped, finger-pressed by the chef,
so if you eat me, I won't fall apart like your night.
What's wrong with your night?
Don't pick the lukewarm sake, which tastes less
seasonal than promotional.
You sit yourself at the far end, alone
as a green tea bag. I gaze at you
every 4.17 minutes, but you're distracted
by my inconvenience of being
round, my groans of being walled by seaweeds.
Tell me there's a connection, a possibility
of choice, even if it's replaceable.
Kids have called me marbles,
but my high-order thinking warns me
I'm not. Meaning gets altered
by context at times. The way I'm orphaned
by a knife gashing my mother's belly.
The way soya sauce spills on your wrist
to varnish the cuts that eat you otherwise.

PRIVATE PARTS

Each of us
an involtini,

the outside rolls
rhetorically
to the inside.

We hang
emotions
like paintings

on our face.
But our face

has revolved:
a safety
box, locked

by a code only
the code knows.

Texture
of privacy tasted
on a forked tongue,

the layered self
on a plate
slain by silver-

ware.

Impossible not to pity the third decimal,
often rounded off, a kind of forced death.
My glasses convex, my chest concave,
ribs growing faster than sternum. A small pool
of sweat forms under the sun, scenery salty,
deformed. On TV, an Oxfam special
about toddlers in rural China: their toe nails
(zoom in) ingrown, their left feet twisted
45 degrees rightward (close-up), like the spiral
roots of strangler figs. Spelling is defective:
the double *e* in *feet* suggests alikeness.
My second language is accessed only with Wi-Fi,
so I speak, mostly, in my mother tongue.
Not much difference between the news
and American home videos: a gum-chewing
pug vs. a gum-chewing president. Humid,
fungi take refuge in books. My back needs
chiropractic treatments after cruising too
long in the crowd for a crown, one that
resembles the Queen's. Call me *majesty*,
forget my skin. Buy me a ticket to Seoul,
where my torso will be altered
to a Rubik's cube. Come to me, my arms
are wide open like those of display watches
forever pointing at 10:10, monogamous
to a temporal angle. Kleptomania claps
in my genes — I've stolen Li Po's title,
but he would not know. Google Search
was not Tang culture. But what culture

do you mean when Wall Street is flooded
with debts and failed specimens of the Me-
generation? Which do you use more often:
iPhone, iPad, or iWords? Is there a word
for the extinction of soap bars and coins?
Why do you want everything liquid, virtual
because it is easier to let go?

OPEN HOUSE

*"Spacious 1554 sq. ft. home with [a] huge dick for entertaining
and enjoying the views..."* — an online property ad

The real estate that was sold like sex
was bought like sex with a typo I did not
not notice. Space was male
when unchallenged, generally not trusting.
Fake was the arboreal décor near the porch,
the half-hackled trunks slumbering from winter
to winter to wince at absences, but what's real
was I, like the seller, also lied: finances,
dreams that failed to cash out, hollowed bridge
loans. And a few visitors.
Body and home were proportioned to not
function. Physical in-coordination was a sign
of overinvestment. I thought
of giving it up, this private space that
gave me possibilities, but fidelity was warm,
meanwhile full of holes. I once
believed in settling, which was only
guaranteed with *buy high, sell higher*. Who could?
Outside, the shadows of trees dwarfed all uniqueness —
the house's, its cement's. My muscles'.
Toes grew to aid *Homo sapiens* to pause
upon walking. The sixth and twelfth ones I had
made a sextant. I gave accurate readings on space.
It did not empty my wallet. The walls did.

A VERY PERSONAL REFLECTION ON MY LESSON
ABOUT *LORD OF THE FLIES*

Pedophiles also love plants.
Mimosa, for example. Or anything that

folds like the skin around the dimples
of these kids. Their flesh so clean, so free
from the trauma of hugs. Rain

pours outside, I think of pineapples

and how my face looks like one.
Instructions: Who said these lines (and in

what context would you say them to me)?
This head is for the beast
It's a gift / You're not wanted
/ The world... slipping away / maybe it's only us /
I painted my face now you eat
and I —

Pages are turned like the body of
a cheap whore, casually but with

expectation. The kids bury their heads
between lines, between thighs, to look for
a remedy for adulthood. How one loses one's

head just by growing up.

Certain
          taboos require a table and a book to sound dirty.

I play a film clip in which a conch
breaks. Calcium is symbolic in its shattering:

you all escape, upon the bell, for vanilla
scoops. I, scopophilic in class with goose-
bumps on my arm, honking.

Blanks in worksheets are bald heads (incl.
mine). Fill them with

hairs.
                              (yours)

A normal heart weighs 350g. Consider living
without one. Organs migrate, have new roles.
Kidneys pumping blood, pancreas counting

pulses, fluidity of grief sluicing forth and
back with lymph — it's called evolution.
The Chinese eat animal viscera, shapes

supplementing shapes. Grilled duck hearts
on skewers, each a pendant, an edible
confinement. What's locked in the four

chambers if not sufferance crispy, sauced,
stories otherwise too cooked to be told.
Leave the heart to the past and the past

to a museum, 3/F, west wing, where it finds
its neighbors, all ill of systole. The hall
savaged by legato vibrato, a soundscape

narrating the pain of being caged too
long by ribs. Long too are the ribs, curving
inward like brackets to brace less and loss.

First the worst: your check
bounced. The primroses sick from
air travel. Me with

a bug swim in swill,
the opening of bleak dreams
calls you lover.

●

I
left, I'm forwarding, there's been
except. A card saying

last, a frying pan,
unaware, burned a
greasy rag like old

noir. I asked these
nippy days to wait, to come
home with less than a

long novella. A
joke: temperature seems to be
dropping new poems.

●

Your family sounds
literary little by
little since last week —

I'll try to get my
keys in cold dumps. A smacking
kiss for my wound, you

in a deck chair
healing yourself in salty
air.

●

That night, your
horror wants to see you hem-
stitching his hope.

The sun is radiant,
is past. The piece: you feel it.
Adolescence was

a major ani-
mator, a looker, under-
done. Here I am, on

the humid ocean,
our faces fade and turn in-
to the tiniest

idea in a
real place.

*

I don't want to hear
lacking. I'm falling

into a bottom-
less pit, the high life doesn't
hear anyone, me.

Lives come in five
volumes, it's quite a task to haul.

*

Me — all water

surrounded by small land
lagoons, oh dear, so well meant.
I have no idea

of how to mend it.
Wild things happen, we behave
like ourselves.

*

A doomed
affair is like bits here and
there, needs editing,

mistakes. I remember
the self — what a shame — holds better
things than the dirt.

●

A Sphinx: that's what you
are, work out for beans, full, fair
and fine, but my

evenings barren
of intercourse. I've seen murders
on the waterfront.

Tonight, I'll worship
heat instead, gnash my teeth, perhaps,
spend ten minutes thinking

the boys, the slums I
like. Love writes part-time. Enter-
taining? Nice? I hope

all is yes.

●

        The beasts
in a city continue
      solitude. There go

      the bells: the pope is
thinking. *May I come live with*
      you again? Nothing

      to explain, obvious:
alone in some dump seems a
      disgrace. Forgive me

      much sooner than next
February. Time hasn't
      been so gloomily

      nice to see.

●

        In your
nacre ears, tension and
      rejection say the

      reverse. It is strange,
quieter than talent above
      a toilet bowl, head

sliding along legs.
"Presentable" may mystify
you.

●

Away from home
a mild attack. Children burn
letters to be sick,

companionless.
Morning coffees teach me how
to talk to strangers.

No no no I mean
insides. Why not, I don't feel
satisfied.

●

I look
daily for a ghost. I want
my new sobbing. I'll

soon be out of arms.
My clock has stopped. I can't leave,
can I? If it were

to have martinis
with you? Enclosed: a head.

●

Come
and come soon, disaster.

I am going to be
you. I paddle the canoe
around the island,

reflectively, I
can. I can too have the
reality.

●

They're
pigs — uncircumscribed poets
believe madly in

breadth, depth, spaciousness,
the atomic brain.

●

Behind
waiting, I mean to

hint on the island
I love other men, imagine
a crumbling of love,

I mean, I mean a
yellow shirt beside him. Is
that pink? Yes. Some more

coffee, if there's not
any left. I like a blank
look passed from face to

face till it litters
the island like leaves. At seven
minutes of seven,

martinis wade the
coast like life.

●

Now rest, my tired
heart. My scalp itches.

Interior in
the state of stirring, so freighted
with meaning, so faint.

It errs, language, its
wit is in its feet and its
feet are in the mud.

Time is creaking like
a cabin on a ship, a
substitute for nothing,

the best part is
nothing is worth barking at
the door. We're going.

•

Another round of
pleasure: cutting a cloud, the
wind detaches (at

last) from a mountain.
I think of James Dean — wasn't
dead — growling at my

navel. A cedar
chest, a few balls, greasy wings.
Isn't real.

•

                                    Off the
cliffs, I keep a residuum,
                a punctured tennis

                ball, half a pair of
scissors, a self-threading needle.
                An angel, the angel

                [   ]
part is true but not the part
                about the human

                voice. Today, ready
to plunge again. I call the
                cats at the museum,

                Grace, my fingers will
be fleet. The weather, black spring.
                The lilacs are going

                to have the tonsils
out.

                        •

                The scale we abandon
                is never right. My

social life skunks,
behaves like an old pillow.
After all, my gaze

is on a diet.
I am thinner. We're breaking.
I know estrangement.

Our egos cross. There's
life lurking in the doorway,
where the treacherous

blue makes delivery.
A lizard asleep under
a geranium

leaf. The street will
devour us.

        ◆

I finally
replace hell with BOYS.

I find an envelope.
It seems to review my hearts.
I can't remember

who told me... it is
big. Unfair, the sky talking
about all this. That

means I could never
think of you. The red eye of
love agrees it is

utter tragedy.
Every time I confront the
mess, I don't know how

long to dig before
admitting defeat. Back stage,
I call for you, Frank.

HOW TO REFUND YOUR IDENTITY

Hang out late

Cover up your feelings at night; always pin or put up your hair as high as
   possible

Reread news that expires in transit

Ribbon your receipt and your self

Spit in the street, a tree, or souring newspapers

Stare at boredom for a corrosive change

Stare at the candlelight or calicobacks in burning fire

Contact manager if your self is on fire. You will be asked to sign in

Think about the imperfection of circles

Roll your eyes often to practice calisthenics of sight

Feed yellowed cabbage to hamsters and munch like them

Make funny jokes or comments on atoms, marbles, or pores

Tell your lover that he is confusing like an ATM operated in a foreign
   language

Pick up history, sprockets, or aversion found on the street

Be nice to all ATMs

Take a sip of bitumen and remember the taste of paved bruises

Shave an anthem in a pond full of butt-upheaving ducks

Leave your bleeding wounds in open air

Listen to the nudity of notes

Find ways to get smaller

LIGHT DEPOSIT

Body as a verb   in
-transitive in / transit   from one
arm to an / other   from

heat to hate   Form a form like
geography / a name   a name
of a city you want to seize / but

doesn't exist   Rub my ear   lobelia or earlobe
that aural peninsular
My clavicle is a bony shore / -line

over-salted / an assault of
alkaline   / I sore   eros I   (also
makes sense in re/verse)   a god body

-ing good deeds / I   a light bug that changes the light
bulb for another light bug   and says
I got your back /   Now bend your

body with jam   and enjambment / Let's
make love recreational   — say —
hopscotch with unnumbered

squares   Your lips tremble   when mine
long / to know where to start   / first

NOTES

"Unspeakable" is a homophonic mistranslation of words and phrases of various languages. It adapts lines from Jean Baudrillard's *Fragments* (Routledge, 2003) and two online articles, "25 Handy Words That Simply Don't Exist in English" and "18 Fantastic Yet Untranslatable Words From Around the Globe," both by Alex Wain.

"Private Parts: American Standard" adapts lines from William Shakespeare's *Macbeth*.

"Trio with Hsia Yü" adapts lines from Hsia Yü's Chinese poetry collection *Ventriloquy* (my own translation).

"Inside Heterosexuality: Notes on Non-Human Resources" adapts a line from Alain de Botton's *How to Think More About Sex* (Picador, 2012).

"Side Effects of Leukemia" adapts lines from Susan Sontag's *Reborn: Journals and Notebooks, 1947-1963* (FSG, 2009) and *Illness as Metaphor and AIDS and Its Metaphors* (Picador, 1999).

"A Very Personal Reflection on My Lesson About Lord of the Flies" adapts lines from William Golding's *Lord of the Flies*.

"Schuyler Haikus, 1954-58" is an erasure of *The Letters of James Schuyler to Frank O'Hara*, edited by William Corbett (Turtle Point Press, 2006).

"How to Refund Your Identity" adapts language from a blog post titled "30 Things You Should Not Do During Hungry Ghost Festival."

"Light Deposit" adapts a line from Xu Xi's *Access* (Signal 8 Press, 2011) and alludes to an image circulated on Facebook, origin unknown.

ACKNOWLEDGEMENTS

Poems in this book have appeared in the following publications (sometimes with changes): *American Letters & Commentary, Asian American Literary Review, Baltimore Review, Bayou, Better: Culture and Lit, Booth, Columbia Poetry Review, The Common, Cream City Review, Desde Hong Kong: Poets in Conversation with Octavio Paz, Harpur Palate, Hawaii Pacific Review, The Journal, La Fovea, Mead: Magazine of Literature and Libations, Minnesota Review, Pank, The Pinch, Pool: A Journal of Poetry, Prism Review, Rhino, Sonora Review, Southern Humanities Review, Superstition Review, Toe Good Poetry, Tupelo Quarterly, Upstreet,* and *World Literature Today.*

Gratitude to Sunyoung Lee, Gerald Maa, Neelanjana Banerjee, Zoë Ruiz, and others from Kaya Press for their hard work on the making of this book and related literary events. I am always indebted to a number of amazing people who have given me guidance and support at different working stages of this collection: Tina Chang, Marilyn Chin, Luis Francia, Ravi Shankar, Xu Xi, Laura McCullough, and Ocean Vuong. Special thanks to Jason Bacasa for his dedication in perfecting the design of the book. "Side Effects of Leukemia" and "MR." are dedicated respectively to Donald Ho (R.I.P.) and my middle school history teacher, K.M. Lai.

I would like to dedicate this book to my family members, regardless of genders and number of legs.

ABOUT THE AUTHOR

Born and educated in Hong Kong, NICHOLAS WONG received his MFA from
City University of Hong Kong and has been a finalist for the New Letters Poetry
Award and the Wabash Prize for Poetry. Described as a "firestarter" by *Time Out:
Hong Kong*, he is an assistant poetry editor for *Drunken Boat*.

KAYA PRESS POETRY

Water Chasing Water, by Koon Woon

Magnetic Refrain, by Nicky Sa-eun Schildkraut

Migritude, by Shailja Patel

Mouth, by Lisa Chen

America & Other Poems, by Nobuo Ayukawa

The Temperature of This Water, by Ishle Yi Park

Tomie's Chair, by Josey Foo

Bridgeable Shores: Selected Poems, by Luis Cabalquinto

The Anchored Angel: Selected Writings, by José Garcia Villa

The Truth In Rented Rooms, by Koon Woon

City Terrace Field Manual, by Sesshu Foster

The Unbearable Heart, by Kimiko Hahn

Premonitions, edited by Walter K. Lew